Mostly MATH

Charles Skidmore
Anne Marie Drayton

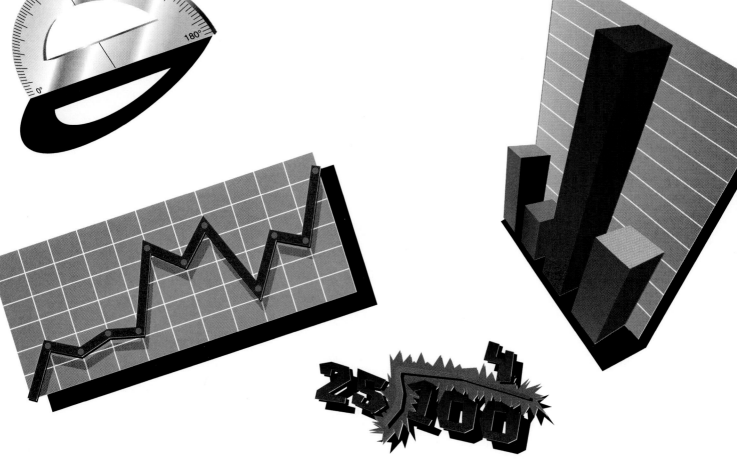

Addison-Wesley Publishing Company

CONTENTS

A Publication of the World Language Division

Director of Product Development
Judith M. Bittinger

Executive Editor
Elinor Chamas

Contributing Writer
Judith M. Bittinger

Editorial Development
Elinor Chamas

Text and Cover Design
Taurins Design Associates

Art Direction and Production
Taurins Design Associates

Production and Manufacturing
James W. Gibbons

Cover art: Andrew Christie
CD ROM Adventures 8–9, 12–13
   Art: Dave Sullivan
   Coloring: Paul Weiner
   Typography: Cliff Garber

Illustrators: Andrew Christie 16–17; Deborah Drummond 2; Ebet Dudley 10 *middle, bottom;* Judy Jarrett 31; Manuel King 27 *top,* 29; Sue Miller 30; Chris Reed 11; Marsha Serafin 14–15; Roni Shepherd 18–19; Jackie Snider 26; Gilles Tibo 20–23.
Photographers: © 1995 M. C. Escher/Cordon Art - Baarn, Holland. All rights reserved.10 *top;* Richard Hutchings 4–6, 28.

ISBN 0-201-54563-2
Mostly Math Softbound
ISBN 0-201-88542-5
Student Book 1 Hardbound (complete)
2 3 4 5 6 7 8 9 10-WC-00 99 98 97

Reading Corner

Try these terrific books!

Eating Fractions by Bruce McMillan
Fun with food and math.

The Doorbell Rang by Pat Hutchins
A funny story about cookies and how to divide them.

Math-a-pedia. by Randall Charles, et al.
Fun visuals in an easy-to-understand math "encyclopedia."

WARM UP DISCARDED

Get started with this graphing activity.

How tall are you?
How many classmates are taller? Shorter? The same?
Make a class height chart and find out.

OBSERVE AND COLLECT DATA ▼

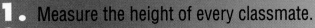

1. Measure the height of every classmate.
2. Make a bar graph.
3. It will look something like this.

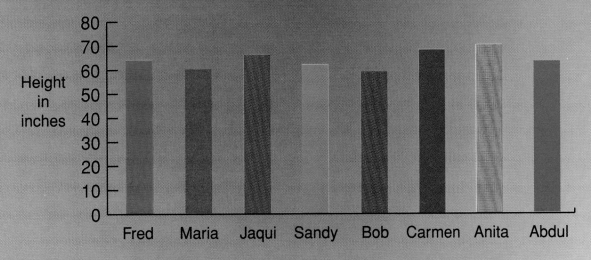

Height in inches

80	
70	
60	
50	
40	
30	
20	
10	
0	

Fred   Maria   Jaqui   Sandy   Bob   Carmen   Anita   Abdul

DRAW CONCLUSIONS ▼

Yes or No?
You are taller than most of your classmates.
You are shorter than most of your classmates.

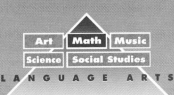

Art Math Music
Science Social Studies

LANGUAGE ARTS

TANGRAM TALES

My brother and I like to play tangrams with our grandfather. Tangrams are a kind of puzzle. Grandfather played tangrams in China.

Art Math Music
Science Social Studies
LANGUAGE ARTS

Grandfather tells us stories to go with the pictures. Some of the stories are about the Fox Fairy. The Fox Fairy can turn into many different animals. He can turn into a huge whale, or a little rabbit.

Fox

Rabbit

Sometimes my brother and I make up our own tangram pictures. Then we ask my parents and my grandfather to guess what they are.

Whale

What do you think this is?

Mostly ∧ Math

Shapes in Flags

Flags use many different shapes and colors. Most often, flags use squares, stripes, triangles, and circles. Describe these flags.

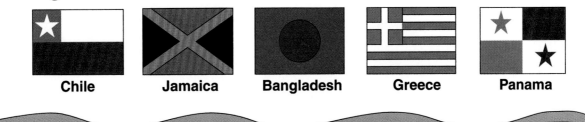

Chile   **Jamaica**   **Bangladesh**   **Greece**   **Panama**

There are many other kinds of flags. The International Flag Code uses a different flag for each letter in the alphabet. Ships use the flags to send messages.

Work with a partner. Describe a flag to your partner. See if your partner can name the letter of the flag you are describing.

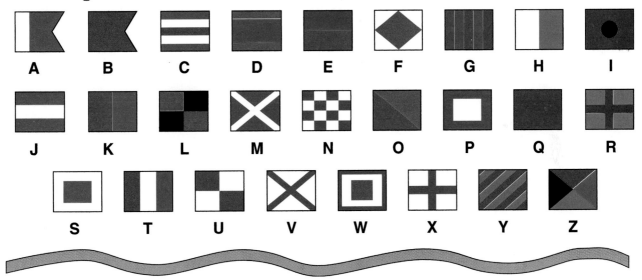

A B C D E F G H I

J K L M N O P Q R

S T U V W X Y Z

Test your flag decoding skills!
Look at each set of flags. What are the messages?

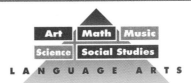

Mostly
∧ Math

A tessellation is an arrangement of figures. The figures fill a flat surface. They do not overlap or leave gaps.

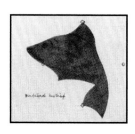

1. How many colors are there?
2. What are the colors in the drawing?
3. How many complete fish are there in the picture?
4. How many incomplete fish?
5. What shapes can you use to make a tessellation?
6. The drawing above is by a famous artist, M.C. Escher. Find out more about him.

The most common tessellation is a tiled floor.

The honeycomb of a hive of bees is also a tessellation.

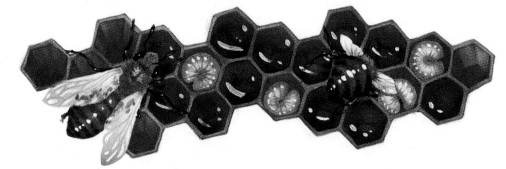

Art Math Music
Science Social Studies
LANGUAGE ARTS

Create Your Own Tessellation

YOU WILL NEED:
- **Scissors, paper, pencil**

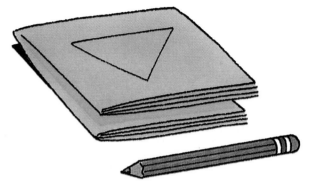

1. Stack two sheets of paper together and fold them twice to make eight layers.

2. Draw a triangle on the top sheet of paper.

 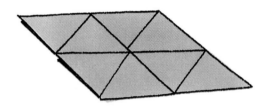

3. Cut the paper so that you get eight identical triangles.

4. Arrange the triangles so that they cover a flat surface.

Repeat the experiment with trapezoids *,*

parallelograms 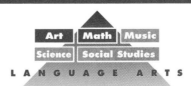 *, and octagons* *.*

Tell which shapes do and don't make tessellations.

Mostly
∧ Math

Art | Math | Music
Science | Social Studies
LANGUAGE ARTS

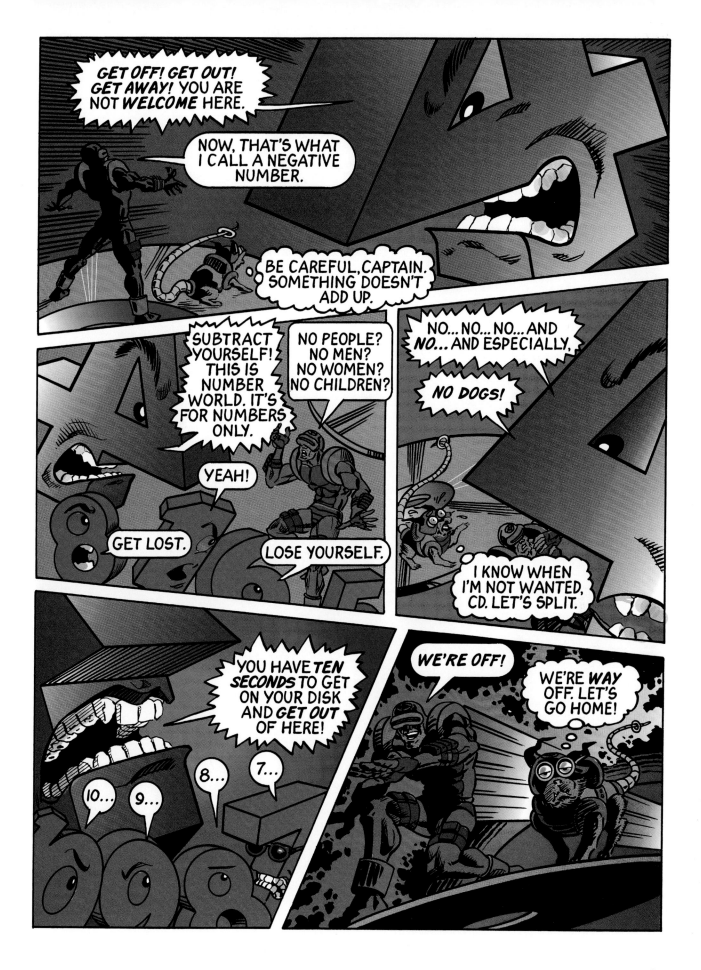

Mike's Munchies

The Main Stuff

Chicken taco	1.29
Corn dog	1.49
Veggie burger	2.99
Giant salad	3.49
Buffalo burger	2.99

The Side Stuff

Cole slaw	1.19
Curly fries	.99
Plantains	1.49
Tomato salad	1.29

The Wet Stuff

	Small	Medium	Large
Soda	.79	.99	1.39
Lemonade	.79	.99	1.39
Iced tea	.79	.99	1.39
Orange Juice	1.19	1.39	1.89
Apple Juice	1.09	1.29	1.69
Milk	.59	.69	.89

The Sweet Stuff

Fruit cup	1.39
Pudding	1.39
Chocolate cake	1.39
Giant cookie	1.39

Art Math Music
Science Social Studies

LANGUAGE ARTS

A. Answer the questions about the menu.

1. Which foods at Mike's restaurant do you like best?
2. How much does a fruit cup cost?
3. How many corn dogs can you buy with $5.00?
4. How much does a small lemonade cost?
5. How many giant cookies can you buy with $4.00?
6. How much does a veggie burger cost?
7. How much do large curly fries cost?
8. How much do all the Sweet Stuff desserts cost?
9. How much does milk cost?
10. How much does it cost to buy a giant salad, curly fries, and a large lemonade?

B. Take four friends to lunch at Mike's. Write down what each person wants. Find the cost of the meal.

C. Imagine you have $5.00. You want to buy one item from each part of the menu — the Main Stuff, The Side Stuff, The Wet Stuff, and the Sweet Stuff. What four items can you afford to buy? Write your answers on another sheet of paper.

WORD

acute angle

obtuse angle

right angle

compass

equation

$$3 \times 5 = 15$$

line segment

angle space formed when two lines meet at a point

area the measure of a region, expressed in square units

calculator a machine that can add, subtract, multiply and divide

centimeter (cm) a unit of length in the metric system. 100 centimeters equal 1 meter

compass an instrument for drawing circles and measuring distance

decimal a number that shows tenths by using a decimal point

division an operation that tells how many times one number is contained in another

equation a number sentence that uses the symbol = (equal)

estimate to find an answer that is close to the exact answer

even number a whole number that has 0, 2, 4, 6, or 8 in the ones place

1.5

decimal point

parallel lines

perpendicular lines

$$\begin{array}{r} 7 \\ + 6 \\ \hline 13 \end{array}$$

addition

$$\begin{array}{r} 25 \\ - 1 \\ \hline 24 \end{array}$$

subtraction

Art Math Music
Science Social Studies
LANGUAGE ARTS

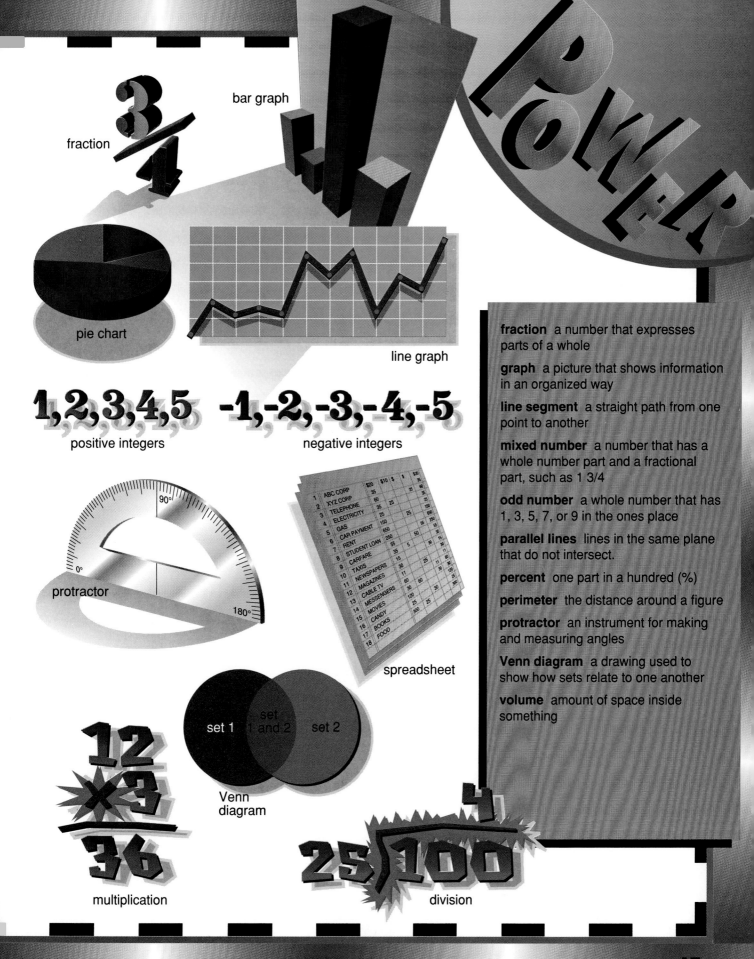

fraction

bar graph

POWER

pie chart

line graph

1,2,3,4,5
positive integers

-1,-2,-3,-4,-5
negative integers

protractor

spreadsheet

12
×3
36
multiplication

Venn
diagram

set 1 set 1 and 2 set 2

25⟌100
division

fraction a number that expresses parts of a whole

graph a picture that shows information in an organized way

line segment a straight path from one point to another

mixed number a number that has a whole number part and a fractional part, such as 1 3/4

odd number a whole number that has 1, 3, 5, 7, or 9 in the ones place

parallel lines lines in the same plane that do not intersect.

percent one part in a hundred (%)

perimeter the distance around a figure

protractor an instrument for making and measuring angles

Venn diagram a drawing used to show how sets relate to one another

volume amount of space inside something

THe HorSe and the DoNKey
A MATH FABLE

A man, a horse, and a donkey were traveling to a distant town. The man loaded all the heavy packages on the donkey's back. He put nothing on the horse's back.

After a few miles the donkey said to the horse, "I'm so tired. These packages are so heavy. Please take one half of the load."

The horse said, "No. I will not carry any packages. I am too handsome for work."

After a few more miles the donkey said to the horse, "I'm so tired. These packages are so heavy. Please take one quarter of the load."

Mostly
∧ Math

Art | Math | Music
Science | Social Studies

LANGUAGE ARTS

"No," answered the horse, "I will not."

"One tenth?" asked the donkey.

"No. No. No. I am far too handsome to carry packages."
Just then the donkey fell down on the ground. The man
understood that the load was too much for the donkey. He
put all the packages on the horse.

Moral: *The strong should help the weak.*

Two Greedy Bears

A FOLKTALE FROM EASTERN EUROPE

Characters: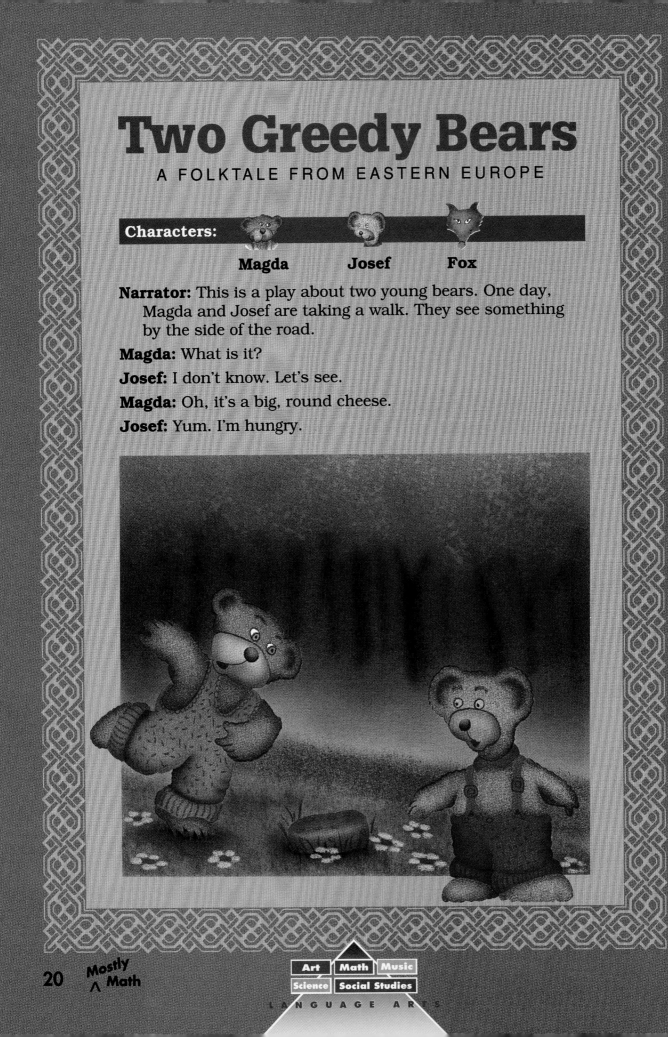

Magda   **Josef**   **Fox**

Narrator: This is a play about two young bears. One day,
Magda and Josef are taking a walk. They see something
by the side of the road.

Magda: What is it?

Josef: I don't know. Let's see.

Magda: Oh, it's a big, round cheese.

Josef: Yum. I'm hungry.

Mostly
∧ Math

Art | Math | Music
Science | Social Studies
LANGUAGE ARTS

Narrator: The greedy bears begin to argue.

Magda: I saw it first. It's mine.

Josef : No, you saw it second. It's mine.

Magda: Give it to me.

Josef: No way - it's mine.

Magda: Look, this is silly. Let's share. You take one-half and I'll take one-half.

Narrator: Josef agrees to share. He breaks the cheese into two pieces. He looks at the two pieces, and he gives one to Magda. But, Magda isn't happy.

Magda: These pieces aren't the same size.

Josef: Yes, they are. These are two equal pieces.

Magda: No, your piece is bigger than my piece.

Josef: It's the *same*.

Narrator: Fox comes out of the woods. He is very hungry. He is also very sly.

Fox: What's the problem?

Magda: Josef's piece of cheese is bigger than mine.

Fox: Give me the cheese. I am a math professor. I can see if you are right.

Narrator: Josef and Magda give Fox the cheese. He holds one piece in each paw.

Fox: I think Josef's cheese is a little bigger. I think that Josef's cheese is 22 ounces. Magda's cheese is only 18 ounces. I can eat a little of Josef's cheese. That will make the two pieces equal.

Magda: Good idea. Eat some of his cheese.

Fox: Just a little ---just a few ounces.

Mostly
∧ Math

Josef: That's too much, Professor. You took about 11 ounces. That was half my cheese. Now Magda has more.

Fox: I see you are a very bright young bear. Well, let me take a little of Magda's cheese.

Magda: That's too much. You ate half my cheese. Now I have only nine ounces and Josef has eleven.

Narrator: The smart fox eats some of Josef's cheese and then some of Magda's cheese. At last there is only a tiny piece for each bear.

Fox: Now your pieces are perfectly equal. They are the same— exactly one ounce each.

Magda: One ounce! That means you ate 38 ounces of cheese!

Josef: That means you ate 95% of our cheese.

Fox: Yes, that's right. And I enjoyed every percent. Next time, don't be so greedy!

A. Answer the questions about the story.

1. Where do Magda and Josef find the cheese?

2. Who sees the cheese first?

3. Why isn't Magda happy with her piece of cheese?

4. What does the Fox say he can do?

5. How does Fox plan to make the two pieces equal?

6. What percent of the cheese does Fox eat?

7. Is Fox sorry that he ate almost all the cheese?

8. Is Fox really a math professor?

B. Complete the analogies. Follow the example.

HUMAN: HAND :: ANIMAL : ____*c. paw*____

    a. bear   b. person   c. paw   d. Josef

1. INCH: FOOT :: OUNCE : _____

    a. cheese   b. yard   c. mile   d. pound

2. HUNGRY: EAT :: THIRSTY : _____

    a. drink   b. fox   c. equal   d. fight

3. ENORMOUS: BIG :: TINY : _____

    a. small   b. heavy   c. equal   d. late

C. The bears argued with each other. Who do you argue with? What do you argue about? Discuss with a partner.

D. This story is a folktale about a fox and two bears. Write as many facts as you know about foxes and bears.

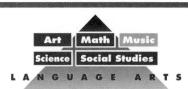

Art   Math   Music

Science   Social Studies

L A N G U A G E   A R T S

Algebra Tiles

YOU WILL NEED:
- Red paper and yellow paper
- Scissors

1. Cut the paper into many small squares.
2. Think of the yellow as positive 1 (+1).
3. Think of the red as negative 1 (-1).
4. Bring together one yellow and one red square.
5. Write down the value as 0.
6. Combine groups of yellow and red squares. Tell what value results.

+1   -1   = 0

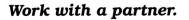

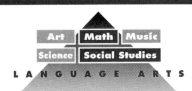

Work with a partner.

1. Show three different ways to have a collection of tiles that represent - 1.
2. Show three different ways to have a collection of tiles that represent 6.
3. Show three different ways to have a collection of tiles that represent - 4.

Paper Money

IT'S EVERYWHERE!

Here's something hard to believe. Paper money doesn't last very long. Dollar bills wear out after about 18 months. The government gets rid of more than 7,000 tons of bills every year. They shred the bills into long strips that look like pasta. Then they shape them into bricks and dump them in landfills.

But landfills are filling up. Some companies are recycling the used-up money in very creative ways. One company takes the shredded bills and rolls them up into fireplace logs! Now people can say "I have money to burn!"

Think Tank

1. **How many dollar bills would you need to fill your classroom?** Here's some information to help you get started. A dollar bill is about 2.6 inches wide and 6 inches long. About 6 dollar bills cover one sheet of typing paper.

2. **Two mothers and two daughters went into an ice-cream shop. They each bought one ice-cream cone. But the store clerk only charged them for three ice-cream cones. Why?**

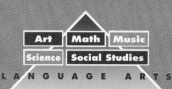

Art   Math   Music
Science   Social Studies
LANGUAGE ARTS

It's a Record!

The furthest a basketball has been dribbled is 265 miles in 14 days.

The record number of table tennis hits in 60 seconds is 172.

The record number of hopscotch games played by one person in one day is 307.

Hank Aaron holds the record for home runs: 755 during his 22-year career.

BULLETIN BOARD

Wanted: Used in line skates.
Size: 10 or 11.
Frankie, Room 68

Math Club Meeting,
Wednesday 3:00 P.M.,
Room 10

Marching Band Practice:
Monday-Wednesday-
Friday: 3:30 P.M. -
Playing Field

Just Joking

Where do fish keep their money?

In a river bank!

Odd or Even Game

Children have been playing math games and counting games for thousands of years. This game comes from ancient Greece.

ODD NUMBERS
1 , 3 , 5 , 7 , 9

EVEN NUMBERS
2 , 4 , 6 , 8 , 10

Number of Players
2 or more

Object of the Game
To get as many markers as possible

Materials needed
- any small markers
  small rocks
  beans
  popcorn kernels
  (unpopped)

How to Play
1. Give each player 15 markers.
2. Have the first person hide some markers in his hand.
3. The first person turns to the second and says, "Odd or Even?"
4. The second person guesses. If the second person is right, she takes the hidden markers. If the second person is wrong, the first person keeps his markers, and play continues. Person 3 asks the next person in the circle, "Odd or even?"

AMAZING FACTS!

● The tallest man on record was Robert Wadlow. He was 8 feet 11 inches tall.

● George Meegan from Great Britain walked 19,019 miles from the southern tip of South America to Northern Alaska. It took him 2,426 days.

● Rick Hansen wheeled his wheelchair over 24,900 miles through four continents and 34 countries.

● There are more than five billion people in the world. If everybody ate a sandwich at the same time on the same day, the sandwiches would reach all the way to the moon and back!

● The longest regularly scheduled bus route in the United States is between Miami, Florida and Los Angeles, California. The route is 2,642 miles and takes 61 hours and 45 minutes.

● Astronauts can "grow" up to 2 inches when they travel in space. When they come back to Earth, they return to their normal height. What makes them shrink? Gravity!

Poetry Corner

Addition

One plus one
is two.
Mother plus father
plus me
is three!
Sisters, brothers, plus
Grandmother Kate
is eight.

How many sisters and brothers do
I have?

Subtraction

Five minus one
is four.
My brother went
away to college,
And now
I have the bedroom
All to myself!

THE WEEKEND

Playing on the weekend, playing with my friends.
Playing on the weekend, hope it never ends.
Playing on the weekend, morning, noon or night –
Monday, it is gone.
Tuesday, it is gone.
Wednesday, it is gone
Thursday, it is gone.
Friday, it is gone.
Monday, Tuesday, Wednesday, Thursday,
Friday, they're all gone, and
It's the weekend!

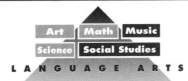

Art Math Music
Science Social Studies
LANGUAGE ARTS

AMAZING FACTS GAME

1 Where are tangrams from?
a. China
b. Korea
c. Canada

2 Which is bigger?
a. one half
b. one quarter
c. one tenth

3 Which is something to eat?
a. menu
b. lemonade
c. corn dog

4 What is true?
a. Magda was a fox.
b. Josef was sad.
c. The fox was smart.

5 How long does a dollar bill last?
a. about 18 years
b. about 18 months
c. about 8 weeks

6 Which is the odd number?
a. 2
b. 3
c. 6

7 What is not a tessellation?
a. a tiled floor
b. a honeycomb
c. a piece of cheese

8 How did Rick Hansen travel?
a. by train
b. by wheelchair
c. by plane

9 What makes astronauts shrink?
a. greedy
b. gravy
c. gravity

Art **Math** Music
Science Social Studies
LANGUAGE ARTS

Mostly Science

Charles Skidmore
Anne Marie Drayton

Addison-Wesley Publishing Company

A Publication of the World Language Division

Director of Product Development
Judith M. Bittinger

Executive Editor
Elinor Chamas

Contributing Writer
Judith M. Bittinger

Editorial Development
Elinor Chamas

Text and Cover Design
Taurins Design Associates

Art Direction and Production
Taurins Design Associates

Production and Manufacturing
James W. Gibbons

Cover art: Andrew Christie
CD ROM Adventures 8–9, 12–13
   Art: Dave Sullivan
   Coloring: Paul Weiner
   Typography: Cliff Garber

Illustrators: Estelle Carol 27, 29; Andrew Christie 16–17, 29; Jim Delapine 7, 14; Deborah Drummond 2, Annie Gusman 31; Gay Holland 5; Judy Jarrett 25; Manuel King 15; Rita Lascaro 18–19, 24; Chris Reed 11; Jackie Snider 26: Chris Spollen 30; Susan Todd 20–23.
Photographer: Wolfgang Bayer/Bruce Coleman Inc. 4; Tom Leeson, Photo Researchers 6; Tom McHugh, Photo Researchers 28.

ISBN 0-201-59977-5
Mostly Science Softbound
ISBN 0-201-88542-5
Student Book 1 Hardbound (complete)
1 2 3 4 5 6 7 8 9 10-WC-00 99 98 97

CONTENTS

Reading Corner

Try these terrific books!

Stiff Ears by Alex Whitney
Animal folk tales from American Indians.

Nature Club and Our Planet by Lionel Bender
Earth facts and photos.

Science Experiments You Can Eat! by Vicki Cobb
Fun "recipes" to follow.

WARM UP

Get started with this growing activity.

OBSERVE AND COLLECT DATA ▼

1. Wet the paper towel. Fold it and put it in the plastic bag.

2. Put three or four beans on top of the paper towel. Seal the bag.

3. Observe the beans each day.

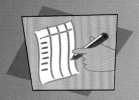

4. Predict how the beans will change.

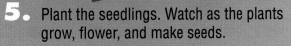

5. Plant the seedlings. Watch as the plants grow, flower, and make seeds.

DRAW CONCLUSIONS ▼

1. What part of a bean's life cycle did you observe? Did your plant make seeds?
2. What might cause a plant's life cycle to end?

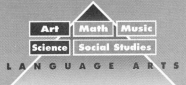

Art Math Music
Science Social Studies
LANGUAGE ARTS

BUSY BEAVERS

Beavers live in a pond. A pond is a water habitat. Many animals and plants live and grow in a habitat.

Beavers build their homes from trees. They chew down the trees with their big front teeth.

A beaver's home is called a lodge. Beavers build their lodges in the middle of ponds.

The lodges have mud floors. The beavers eat and sleep on the mud floor.

Beavers eat leaves and tree bark. They store tree branches at the bottom of the pond. These branches are food for the winter.

Mostly
∧ Science

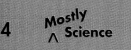

Art · Math · Music
Science · Social Studies

LANGUAGE ART

When the top of the pond freezes over, beavers bring the branches into their lodge. If all the pond freezes, beavers still have food. They eat the walls of their lodge!

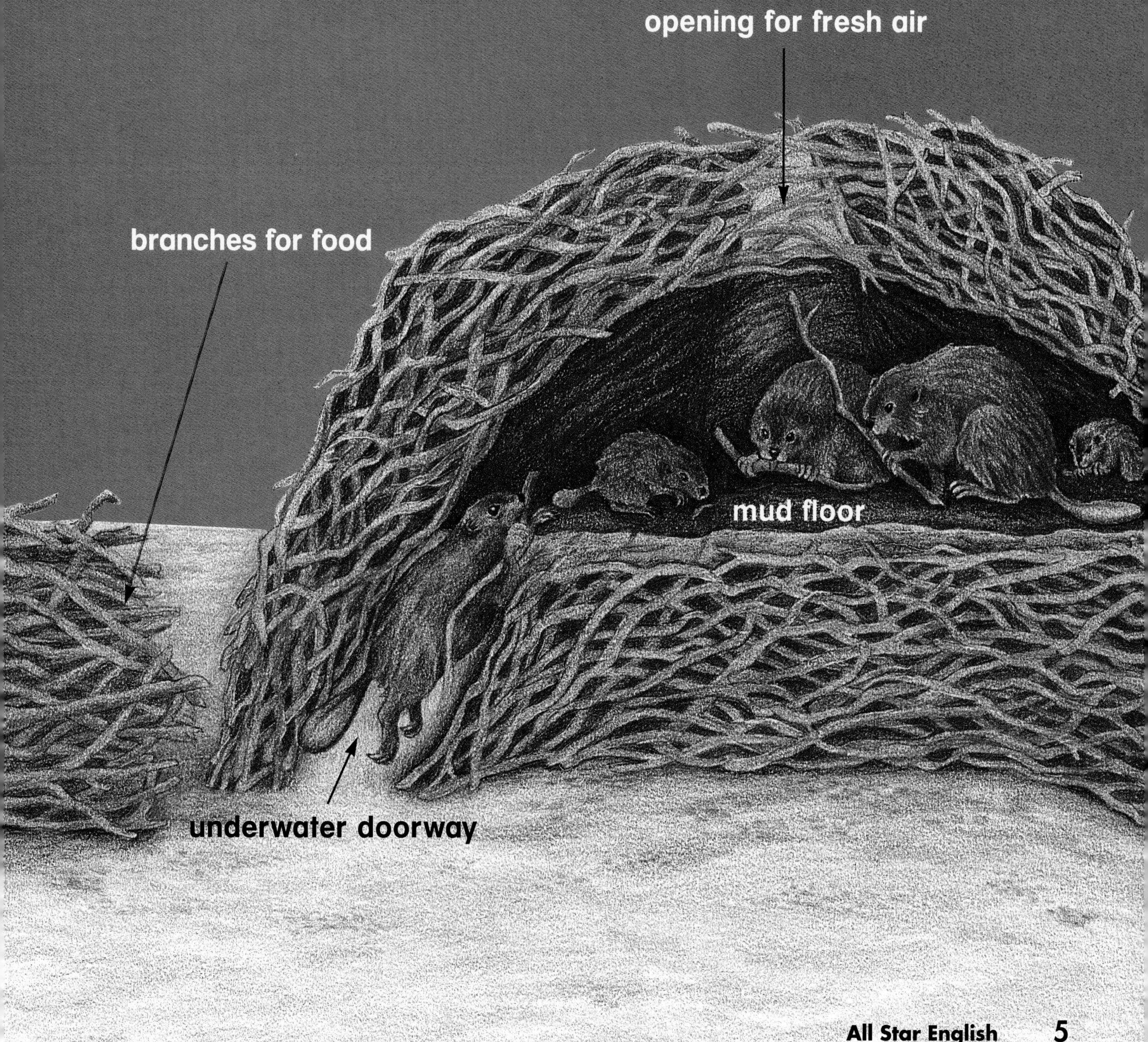

opening for fresh air

branches for food

mud floor

underwater doorway

Beavers are good swimmers. Baby beavers learn how to swim when they are only a few days old. When a beaver sees danger, it slaps its wide tail against the water. That makes a loud noise. The other beavers dive quickly under the water. They are safe in their lodge.

Beavers talk to each other. They rub noses, make soft sounds, and whistle.

What other animals are part of a pond habitat?

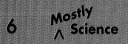

Totems

The Haida Indians lived in the Pacific Northwest. They used the giant trees of the forest to build their homes and canoes. They also carved totem poles. They carved faces of owls, frogs, bears, beavers, eagles, and many other creatures. The animals told a story about the family that carved the pole.

Line Symmetry

Symmetry means "the same on both sides." Look at the thunderbird. This symbol is used in American Indian art, especially art from the Pacific Northwest. Does it have symmetry? How many lines of symmetry are there?

A magnet can pull many things. Feel the pull of a magnet.
What can your magnet pull?

OBSERVE AND COLLECT DATA ▼

Try these things.		YES	NO
a penny			
paper clips			
scissors			
pencils			
a dime			
a string			
a crayon			
paper			
a jar lid			

Art   Math   Music
Science   Social Studies
LANGUAGE ARTS

Make Magnetic Sailboats

YOU WILL NEED:
- plastic tray
- a magnet
- pins
- tape
- ruler
- paper
- thin sheet of foam or cork

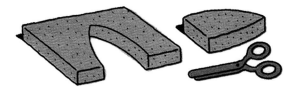

1. Cut some boat shapes from the foam or cork.

2. Push three or four pins into each boat.

3. Push one pin vertically into each. This is the mast.

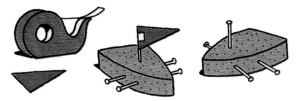

4. Cut out paper sails and tape them to the masts.

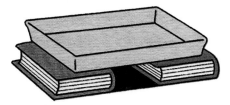

5. Place the tray on two boxes or piles of books.

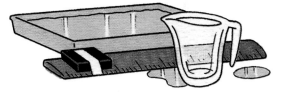

6. Tape the magnet to the ruler. Pour some water into the tray. Make some islands if you like.

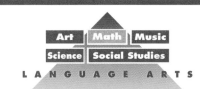

7. Move the magnet under the tray. Have races with your friends.

Mostly
∧ Science

Art | Math | Music
Science | Social Studies
LANGUAGE ARTS

Favorite Sounds

What's your favorite sound? Juan Verde likes the sound of rain falling on a roof. Marie Rousseau likes the sound of a piano. Han Vi loves the sound of a bells ringing from a tower. Many people have favorite sounds. But even the sound you like best will hurt your ears if it is too loud.

Scientists measure sounds in decibels. One decibel is very small. A whisper is 20 decibels. Your speaking voice is usually about 60 decibels. Look at the following chart to see other sounds and their decibel levels.

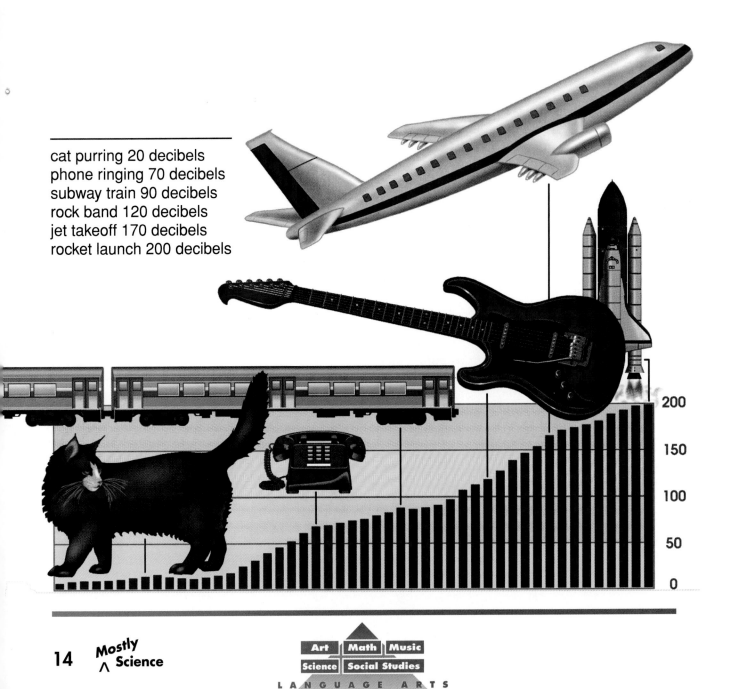

cat purring 20 decibels
phone ringing 70 decibels
subway train 90 decibels
rock band 120 decibels
jet takeoff 170 decibels
rocket launch 200 decibels

200
150
100
50
0

Art   Math   Music
Science   Social Studies

LANGUAGE ARTS

Answer the following questions about sound.

1. Which sound is louder – a rock band or a telephone ringing?
2. Which sound is softer – a whisper or a moving subway train?
3. Which sound is louder – a jet takeoff or a rocket launch?
4. Which sound is softer – a phone ringing or a normal speaking voice?
5. Which sound is louder – a jet taking off or a rock band?

*Look at the following pictures. Make **louder than** or **softer than** statements about each set of pictures. Follow the example.*

EXAMPLE:

Example: A siren is louder than a doorbell.

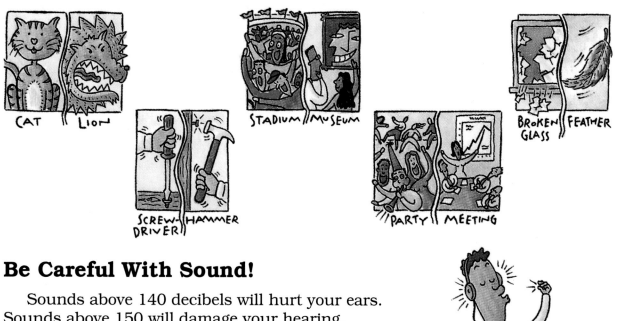

Be Careful With Sound!

Sounds above 140 decibels will hurt your ears. Sounds above 150 will damage your hearing. Constant exposure to sounds over 85 or 90 decibels can also damage your hearing. Be careful of your ears. Don't listen to loud music!

WORD

LIFE CYCLE

growing

dying

sprouting

seed

asteroid a rock in space, usually found in an area between Mars and Jupiter

atmosphere the air around the earth

atom the smallest particle of any kind of matter

axis the imaginary line around which an object rotates or spins

carbon dioxide a colorless, odorless gas that makes up part of the air

comet a ball of ice that orbits the Sun and has a long tail when close to the Sun

data pieces of information or facts

element a substance made of only one kind of atom

Earth the planet we live on

experiment a test to try to find out something or to prove an idea

laboratory a room or building where science experiments are done

life cycle the pattern of growing, reproducing, and dying

machine a thing that makes it easier to do work

atmosphere

crust

PLANET EARTH

mantle

inner core

Art | Math | Music
Science | Social Studies
LANGUAGE AR

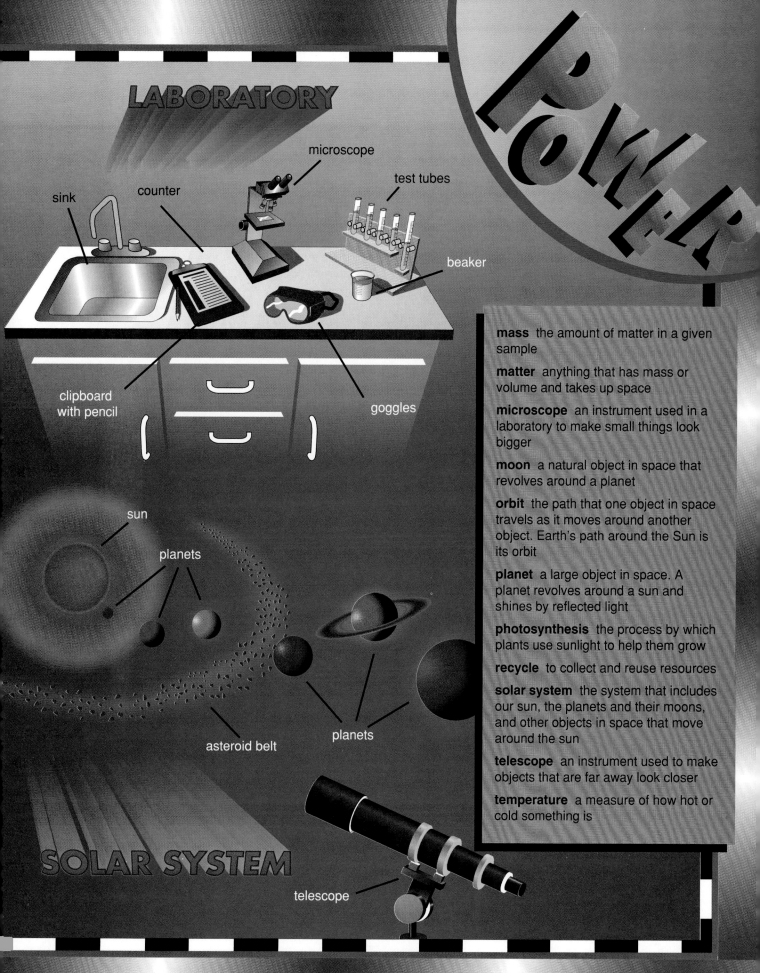

LABORATORY

sink

counter

microscope

test tubes

beaker

clipboard
with pencil

goggles

POWER

mass the amount of matter in a given sample

matter anything that has mass or volume and takes up space

microscope an instrument used in a laboratory to make small things look bigger

moon a natural object in space that revolves around a planet

orbit the path that one object in space travels as it moves around another object. Earth's path around the Sun is its orbit

planet a large object in space. A planet revolves around a sun and shines by reflected light

photosynthesis the process by which plants use sunlight to help them grow

recycle to collect and reuse resources

solar system the system that includes our sun, the planets and their moons, and other objects in space that move around the sun

telescope an instrument used to make objects that are far away look closer

temperature a measure of how hot or cold something is

sun

planets

asteroid belt

planets

SOLAR SYSTEM

telescope

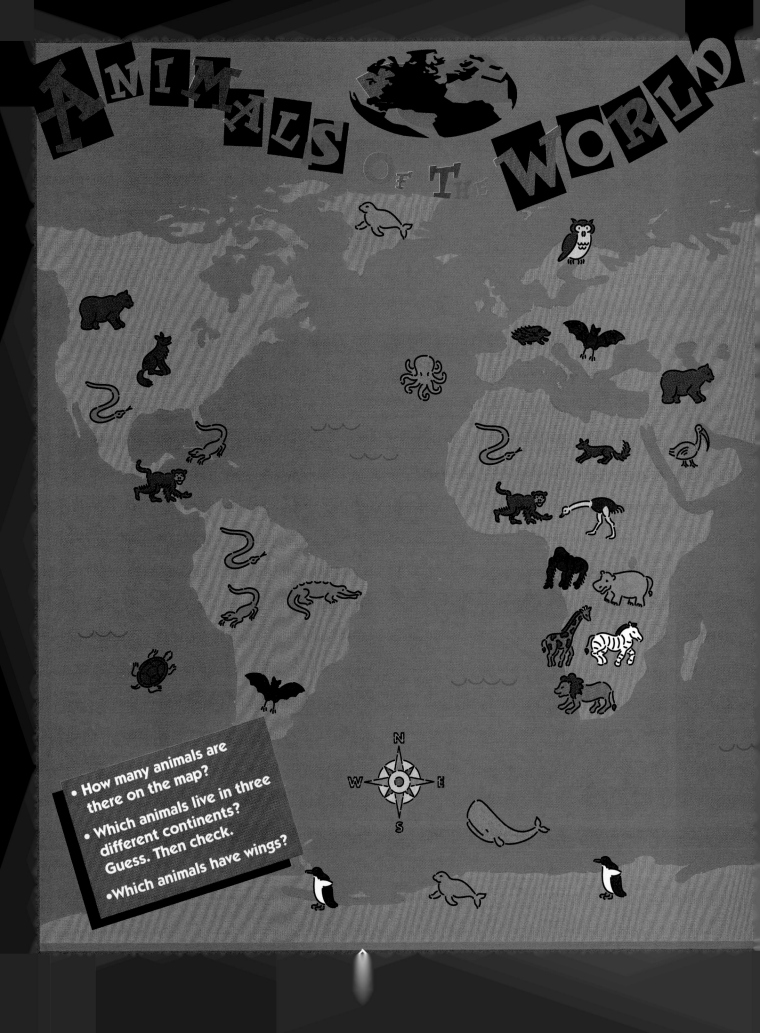

ANIMALS OF THE WORLD

- How many animals are there on the map?
- Which animals live in three different continents? Guess. Then check.
- Which animals have wings?

	AFRICA	THE AMERICAS	ANTARCTICA	ASIA	AUSTRALIA	EUROPE
bat	●	●		●	●	●
bear	●	●		●		●
camel	●			●		
crocodile	●	●			●	
dolphin	●	●		●	●	●
elephant	●			●		
fox	●	●				●
giraffe	●					
gorilla	●					
hedgehog	●					●
hippo	●					
kangaroo					●	
lion	●			●		
lizard	●	●		●	●	●
monkey	●	●		●		
octopus						
ostrich	●					
owl	●	●		●		●
panda				●		
pelican	●	●			●	
penguin		●	●		●	
rhinoceros	●			●		
seal	●	●	●	●	●	●
shark	●	●	●	●	●	●
snake	●	●		●	●	●
tiger				●		
turtle	●	●		●	●	●
whale	●	●	●	●	●	●
wolf	●	●		●		●
zebra	●					

TALK IT OVER

- Work with a friend. Think of an animal. Ask your friend to guess the animal.

- Is it brown?
- Does it have legs?
- Does it live in Africa?

How Coyote Placed the Stars

A WASCO INDIAN LEGEND

Long, long ago, a coyote lived in the desert. Every night he looked up at the night sky. He liked to watch the stars shine in the dark.

One night, Coyote and his friend Bear were star watching. Coyote had an idea. "I'm tired of the desert. I think I'll climb to the sky."

Mostly
∧ Science

Art | Math | Music
Science | Social Studies
LANGUAGE ARTS

Bear scratched his big head. "How can you do that?"

"No problem," Coyote said. "I'll use my bow and arrows."

Coyote got a large pile or arrows. He shot them into the sky. The first arrow flew far into the night. It landed on the moon. Coyote shot a second arrow. It caught in the notch of the first. Coyote shot many more arrows until they made a ladder.

Coyote began to climb. He climbed higher and higher. Finally, he reached the moon. He was happy there. He was happier there than on earth. But then he got another idea.

"I wonder if I can move the stars around with my arrows?" His first arrow hit a star. The star moved across the sky. He shot another arrow...and another...until the stars were arranged in the shape of a coyote. Coyote thought of his friend Bear. He arranged some stars in the form of a bear.

Mostly
∧ Science

Coyote worked all night. He made outlines of all his friends – Mountain Lion, Horse, Goat, Fish, Owl, and Eagle. Then he admired his work. The sky was full of new constellations.

A. Answer the following questions about the story.

1. Where did Coyote live?

2. What did Coyote look at every night?

3. Why did Coyote decide to climb to the sky?

4. How did Coyote make a ladder to the moon?

5. How did Coyote feel when he got to the moon?

6. What idea did Coyote get when he was on the moon?

7. What were the first two animal outlines Coyote made?

8. What do we call these outlines in the sky?

B. Think About It

Many Native Americans told stories about Coyote. They thought that the coyote was a smart and tricky animal. Think about the following animals. What kind of personalities do they have?

elephant   owl   monkey   snake

Talk about other animals that you know about. What kind of personalities do those animals have?

C. Draw the sky as it looked after Coyote finished his work. Then draw another sky with the constellations you would like to see in the sky. Present your work to the class.

D. Find information about the following constellations at your school library: Ursa Major, Gemini, Cygnus, Hydra.

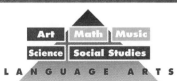

The Solar System

The sun and all the things in orbit around it are called the solar system. Make a model of the solar system. It will help you understand just how big it really is. All you need are ten popsicle sticks or tongue depressors. Take them to a park or playground with your friends.

Write the names of all the planets and the sun on the sticks. Push the stick with the name of the sun on it into the ground. Then, starting from the sun each time, put all the other sticks around it like this:

Pluto
42 big steps away

Neptune
32 big steps away

Uranus
21 big steps away

Saturn
ten big
steps away

Jupiter
five big steps away

Mars one and a half steps away
Earth one big step away
Venus three-quarters of a step away
Mercury half a step away

Sun

Art Math Music
Science Social Studies
LANGUAGE ARTS

UFO ALERT

An airplane pilot in Washington state looked up in surprise on June 24, 1947. He saw strange-looking things in the sky. He said they were moving like saucers skipping over the water. That's why we call UFOs "flying saucers!"

RING AROUND SATURN

Thousands of rings orbit Saturn. They might be made of dust and rocks or pieces of a moon that broke apart. Some chunks are as small as a button —and some are bigger than a house!

Star Struck

Stars look white to us, but they're not! The hottest stars are really blue. The coolest stars are really red!

Have you ever wished on a star at night? You can also wish on a star during the day. That's because the sun is really a star! The sun is the brightest star you see. Why? It is the star nearest the earth.

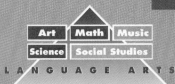

Art | Math | Music
Science | Social Studies
LANGUAGE ARTS

ONE WEIRD PLANET

Would you like to spend your vacation on Uranus? Summer lasts 21 years there! But you can't get a suntan. The average temperature is 300 degrees below zero (F).

BULLETIN BOARD

Lost: Math and Science Journal. It's covered in green paper. My name is in it. Please return it! Carlos, Room 18

Needed: Help in the library. Come and see me. Mrs. Lee

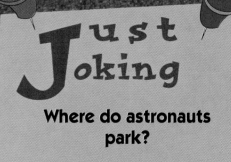

Just Joking

Where do astronauts park?

♦♦♦♦♦

At parking meteors!

♦♦♦♦♦

Creepy Crawly Things

Insects are the most common type of animal in the world. Insects are creatures with six legs and three body parts. The three body parts are the head, the thorax and the abdomen. About 99.9 percent of all insects have wings.

Spiders are not insects; they are insects' enemies. Spiders are arachnids. They have four pairs of legs, two body parts, and no antennae. Spiders live everywhere in the world except Antarctica. About half of all spiders catch insects for food in their webs.

There are about 4000 different kinds of mammals on the planet earth. How many different kinds of insects are on the earth?

10 MILLION

9 MILLION

8 MILLION

7 MILLION

6 MILLION

5 MILLION

4 MILLION

3 MILLION

2 MILLION

1 MILLION

4 THOUSAND

AMAZING FACTS!

- What's the biggest school in the whole world? A school of herring. One school of herring can contain hundreds of millions of fish.

- In 1995, an auto mechanic in Argentina found some dinosaur fossils. The dinosaur was alive about 100 million years ago! The beast was 41 feet long and weighed about six tons!

- An anteater sticks its tongue in and out 100 times a minute to slurp up its food.

- Snowflakes come in many, many shapes. No two are exactly alike. Snowflakes have line symmetry. They have six sides. What other things have 6 sides? What do we call a six-sided figure in math?

Poetry Corner

A Trip to Space

SOPHIE HAGMAN

I'm going to build a spaceship
Just big enough for me;
I'll fly around the planets,
To see what I can see.

Maybe I'll go to Saturn,
And zoom around its rings;
Or land on a moonbeam,
And get some rocks and things.

I'll say hello to Venus,
And flash around the sun;
I'll float in my space suit.
I'll have a lot of fun.

I'll rest in the Milky Way,
And have myself a snack;
I'll wave to planet Jupiter,
And then I'll come right back!

30   Mostly
     ∧ Science

LISTEN TO THE RAINDROPS

BY BOB SCHNEIDER

Chorus
Listen to the raindrops falling down;
Listen to the raindrops on the ground;
Listen to the raindrops falling down,
Falling down.

1st Verse
Now, I look outside my window,
And I smell the fresh, clean air;
The trees, they sway so gently;
And the mist lies everywhere;
And it feels so good just
To hear the sound so clear,
As we...

2nd Verse
Now in the city or the country,
You could be sitting on the back porch stairs;
Friends and family around you
So silently aware –
As you sit and watch
And hear the sound so clear,
As you...

(Chorus)

AMAZING FACTS GAME

EACH SQUARE =
5 POINTS

THREE IN A ROW =
10 BONUS POINTS

1 Which word means "the same on both sides?"
a. silently
b. shock
c. symmetry

2 What is the most common type of animal?
a. mammals
b. spiders
c. insects

3 What is a beaver's home called?
a. a lodge
b. a pond
c. a habitat

4 Which of these will a magnet pull?
a. a crayon
b. a penny
c. a string

5 Which has six sides?
a. a snowflake
b. a square
c. a triangle

6 What is the brightest star in the sky?
a. Venus
b. the moon
c. the sun

7 The sound of a subway train measures . . .
a. 20 decibels
b. 90 decibels
c. 200 decibels

8 The hottest stars are
a. blue
b. red
c. yellow

9 Spiders live everywhere but...
a. Africa
b. Antarctica
c. America

32 Mostly
∧ Science

Art Math Music
Science Social Studies
L A N G U A G E   A R T S

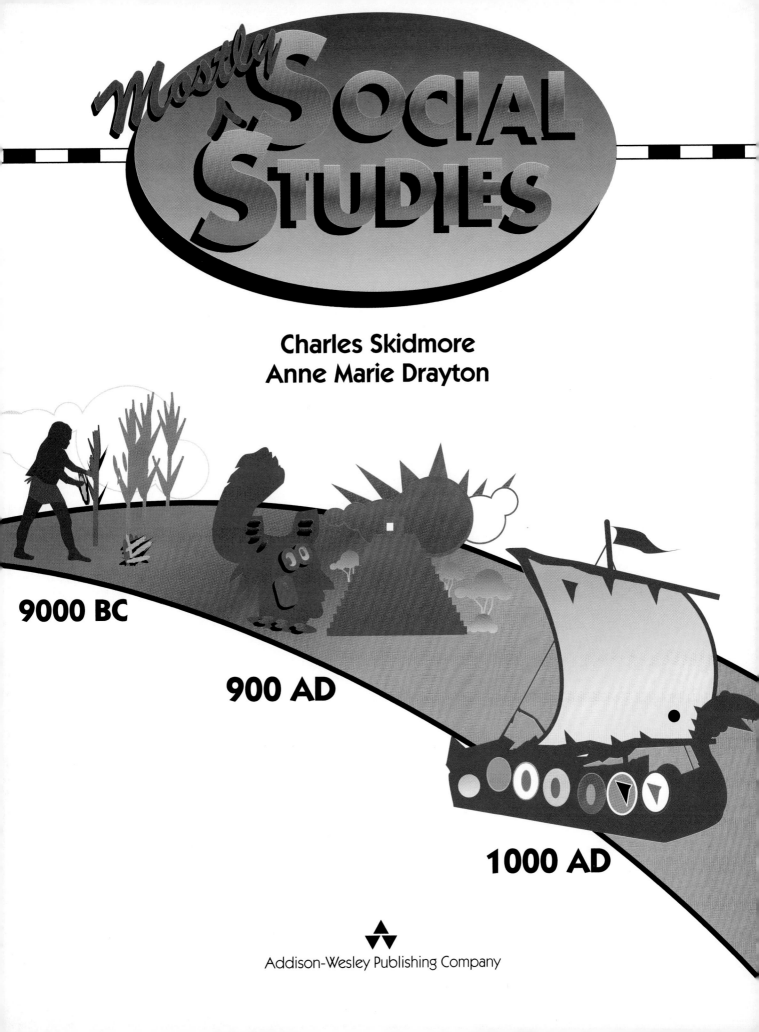

Mostly SOCIAL STUDIES

Charles Skidmore
Anne Marie Drayton

9000 BC

900 AD

1000 AD

Addison-Wesley Publishing Company

A Publication of the World Language Division

Director of Product Development
Judith M. Bittinger

Executive Editor
Elinor Chamas

Contributing Writer
Judith M. Bittinger

Editorial Development
Elinor Chamas

Text and Cover Design
Taurins Design Associates

Art Direction and Production
Taurins Design Associates

Production and Manufacturing
James W. Gibbons

Cover art: Chris Spollen
CD ROM Adventures 8–9, 12–13
  Art: Dave Sullivan
  Coloring: Paul Weiner
  Typography: Cliff Garber

Illustrators: Estelle Carol 28; Andrew Christie 16–17; Danuta Jarecka 30; Deborah Pinkney 31; Chris Reed 11, 25; Vera Rosenberry 20–23; Neil Shigley 18–19; Jackie Snider 26; Chris Spollen 7, 14–15.
Photographers: Ron Edmonds, AP/Wide World Photos 10 *middle*; Richard Hutchings 2, 4–5; Russell McPhedran, AP/Wide World Photos 29 *right;* Vee Inthaly 6; Richard Strauss, Smithsonian Institution, Courtesy the Supreme Court of the United States 10 *bottom;* Wide World Photos 10 *top,* 29 *left.*

ISBN 0-201-59979-1
Mostly Social Studies Softbound
ISBN 0-201-88542-5
Student Book 1 Hardbound (complete)
2 3 4 5 6 7 8 9 10-WC-00 99 98 97

CONTENTS

Reading Corner
Try these terrific books!

Visual Geography by Lerner.
27 books loaded with fun facts.

The Fire Bringer by Margaret Hodges
An Indian boy and a coyote bring fire to the prairie.

The Giving Tree by Shel Silverstein
About the give and take of friendship.

WARM UP

Get started with this project.

What's the story behind your first name?
Talk to your family. Find out the story.

OBSERVE AND COLLECT DATA ▼

1. Who gave you your name?

2. Why did they choose that name?

3. Write down the story and make a name poster.

SAIDEH

My name is Saideh. My mom chose my name. She thinks it's the best name in the world. Saideh means "lucky" in Arabic, so I think I will always have good luck.

Art Math Music
Science Social Studies

LANGUAGE ARTS

GETTING TO KNOW YOU

VIETNAM

Phuong Mai Nguyen
Vietnam

I'm from Vietnam. Vietnam is in Asia. It is sunny and warm. Children like to ride their bicycles and play games. My favorite foods were oranges, bananas, and ice cream.

My first day of school in the United States was good. A student named Melvin helped me. He showed me what to do. We played basketball. I learned about the days of the week and the months of the year. I'm interested in music.

MEXICO

Francisco Hernandez
Mexico

I'm from Mexico. My grandmother still lives in Mexico. She lives in Guadalajara. I miss her.

In Mexico, it is hot. There are lots of things to do there. You can play soccer. You can sing songs and dance. We have good food in Mexico. I like tacos, rice, and refried beans. I'm interested in Native Americans.

4 Mostly
∧ Social Studies

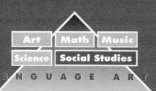

Art | Math | Music
Science | Social Studies
LANGUAGE ARTS

NICARAGUA

Alphonso Alvarez
Nicaragua

I am from Central America. My country is Nicaragua. It is a country with two sea coasts--like the United States. The east coast is on the Caribbean Sea. The west coast is on the Pacific Ocean. I am from the capital city, Managua.

It is very hot in Nicaragua. It was too hot after noon time to be in school. My school started at 7:00 and ended at 12:00. I'm interested in geography.

PHILIPPINES

Lorenca Sabiniano
Philippines

I'm from the Philippines. They are islands in the Pacific Ocean. There are about 7,000 islands in the Philippines!

I came to America with my parents. My grandparents live in Baguio with my aunt. I have a new sister. She is fat and cute. She likes to cry and eat and sleep. I'm interested in government.

HAITI

Dominique Cazeau
Haiti

I'm from Haiti. Haiti is in the Caribbean. It is warm and sunny on my island. The Dominican Republic is on the same island as Haiti.

I had a wonderful dog in Haiti. His name was Hamilton. I liked to work in my vegetable garden when I was in Haiti. I'm interested in computers.

BACi

A STUDENT MEMORY
AS TOLD TO JOHN MUNDAHL

Lao people
Have the Baci Ceremony.
We use string.

We tie the string around the wrist
Of an honored person.

Like this:

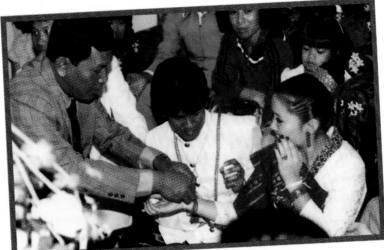

Wedding ceremony of Vee Inthaly

Honored people are:
People getting married.
Guests in your house.
People taking a trip.
People graduating from school.
Can you think of others?

The string is worn for three days.
It's a sign of friendship.

American Holidays

Most American holidays honor famous people or events in American history. The holidays tell the story of our country.

Independence Day - This holiday, July 4, celebrates America's declaration of independence from England in 1776.

Labor Day - This day celebrates the American worker. It is the first Monday in September.

Martin Luther King Day - This holiday celebrates the man who helped African Americans get equal rights in the United States.

Presidents' Day - George Washington and Abraham Lincoln were both born in February. They were both great presidents. This holiday celebrates the birthdays of these two famous men.

Veterans' Day - This holiday, November 11, honors all men and women who fought in American wars.

Thanksgiving Day - Thanksgiving is another November holiday. It is celebrated on the fourth Thursday of November. Early settlers in the Americas gave thanks for a good life in the New World. Americans still spend one day each year in thanks for the good life they have in the United States.

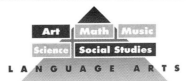

The United States government has three branches. The branches are the executive, the legislative, and the judicial. People in different branches have different jobs.

The Executive Branch: the President, the Vice-President, and the President's Cabinet. They carry out the laws.

The White House

Congress in session

The Legislative Branch: the members of the House of Representatives and the Senate, or Congress. Congress passes the laws.

The Judicial Branch: the judges. They decide if the laws are constitutional.

The Justices of the Supreme Court

Native Americans

Millions of Native Americans lived in North and South America long before 1492. They were here before Christopher Columbus. There were over 2,000 different languages and cultures on these two continents.

Look at the time line. It shows some important events in Native American history.

3,000 BC
Native Americans used metals for weapons

250 AD
Mayans began to build great pyramids and temples

40,000-20,000 BC
Asian hunters crossed into North America

100 AD
Anasazi Civilization began to grow in American Southwest

9,000-7,000 BC
Native Americans began to grow crops

Answer the questions below in complete sentences.

1. When did the Asian hunters cross into North America?
2. What did the Mayans begin to build in 250?
3. When did Columbus reach the Americas?
4. What happened around 9,000 B.C.?
5. When did the Vikings sail to present-day Canada?
6. When did the Anasazi Civilization begin to grow?
7. When did Montezuma rule the Aztecs?
8. When did the population of Tikal reach 100,000?

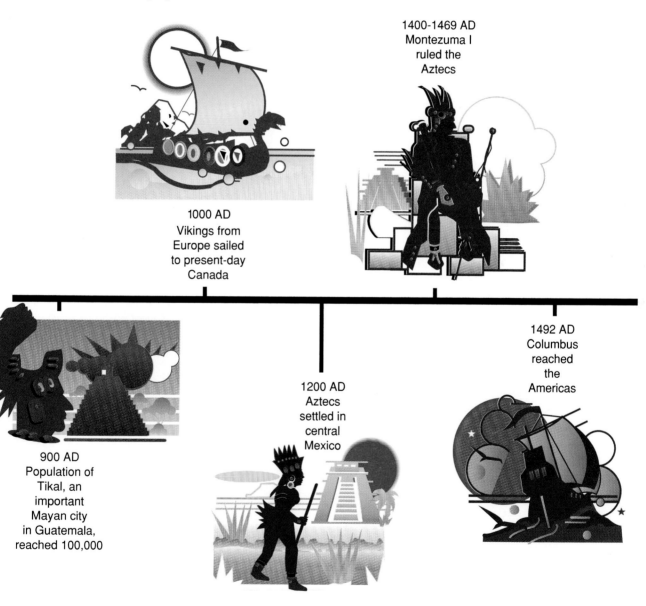

1400-1469 AD
Montezuma I
ruled the
Aztecs

1000 AD
Vikings from
Europe sailed
to present-day
Canada

900 AD
Population of
Tikal, an
important
Mayan city
in Guatemala,
reached 100,000

1200 AD
Aztecs
settled in
central
Mexico

1492 AD
Columbus
reached
the
Americas

WORD

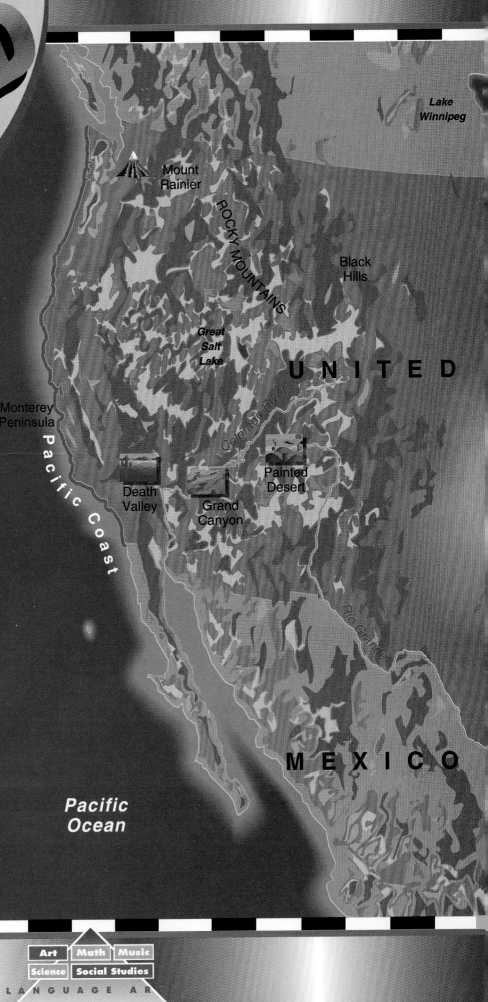

bay an inlet of the sea smaller than a gulf. Where on the map is San Francisco Bay?

cape land that sticks out into water. Cape Cod is in Massachusetts. Where is Cape Cod Bay? Where in the world is the Cape of Good Hope?

coast the land near an ocean or sea. Which of the United States are on the Pacific Coast?

continent one of seven great divisions of land on the globe. Can you name the seven continents?

desert wild, arid land with little or no water. Where in the world is the Sahara Desert?

forest land covered with trees and underbrush. A forest is like a woods, but bigger. Which part of the U. S. has the most forests and woods?

gulf a part of an ocean or sea extending into the land. Where in the world is the Gulf of Mexico? Where is the Persian Gulf?

island land surrounded by water. An island is smaller than a continent. Where in the world are the Hawaiian Islands? The Philippines?

Lake
Winnipeg

Mount
Rainier

ROCKY MOUNTAINS

Black
Hills

Great
Salt
Lake

U N I T E D

Monterey
Peninsula

Colorado River

Pacific Coast

Painted
Desert

Death
Valley

Grand
Canyon

Rio Grande

M E X I C O

Pacific
Ocean

Art Math Music
Science Social Studies

L A N G U A G E   A R

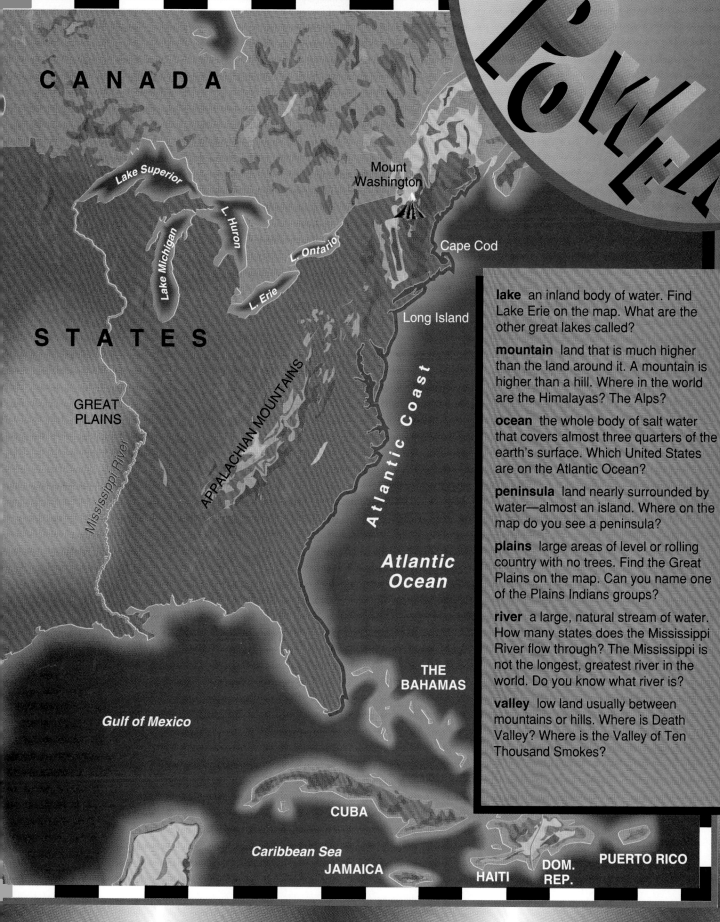

CANADA

Lake Superior

L. Huron

Lake Michigan

L. Ontario

L. Erie

Mount Washington

Cape Cod

Long Island

STATES

GREAT PLAINS

APPALACHIAN MOUNTAINS

Mississippi River

Atlantic Coast

Atlantic Ocean

THE BAHAMAS

Gulf of Mexico

CUBA

Caribbean Sea

JAMAICA

HAITI

DOM. REP.

PUERTO RICO

lake an inland body of water. Find Lake Erie on the map. What are the other great lakes called?

mountain land that is much higher than the land around it. A mountain is higher than a hill. Where in the world are the Himalayas? The Alps?

ocean the whole body of salt water that covers almost three quarters of the earth's surface. Which United States are on the Atlantic Ocean?

peninsula land nearly surrounded by water—almost an island. Where on the map do you see a peninsula?

plains large areas of level or rolling country with no trees. Find the Great Plains on the map. Can you name one of the Plains Indians groups?

river a large, natural stream of water. How many states does the Mississippi River flow through? The Mississippi is not the longest, greatest river in the world. Do you know what river is?

valley low land usually between mountains or hills. Where is Death Valley? Where is the Valley of Ten Thousand Smokes?

PHAETON AND THE CHARIOT OF THE SUN

Long ago, people in Greece told stories about the gods. Apollo was the god of the sun. He kept the sun in a beautiful chariot. Every morning Apollo drove the chariot across the sky. The people on earth watched the sun move from east to west.

Apollo had a son named Phaeton. One day, Phaeton said, "Please, let *me* drive the chariot across the sky."

"Oh, no, Phaeton," Apollo answered. "You cannot drive the chariot of the sun. The horses are too big and strong. You cannot control them. If you go too high, the earth will be too cold. If you go too low, the earth will burn."

Phaeton didn't listen. The next morning he took the chariot and the four big horses and started across the sky. But the horses were too strong. Phaeton could not control them. First they ran up high into the sky. On Earth, snow fell and ice formed. Then the chariot went down very fast. Part of the earth began to burn. Deserts formed and lakes dried up.

Art | Math | Music
Science | Social Studies
LANGUAGE ARTS

Zeus, the King of the gods, looked down and saw what was happening. He took his lightning bolt and shot it at Phaeton. Phaeton fell into the sea and died. But it was too late to change the earth. That is why we have different land forms and different weather.

Presents for America

Long ago, there was a man named John Chapman. He lived in the state of Massachusetts. He loved the outdoors. He loved the forests and the hills. He loved the rivers and the lakes. He loved all the wild animals.

John Chapman spent a lot of time outdoors. One day, he was walking in the woods. He stopped to rest and to eat an apple. Then he looked at the apple seeds in his hands. He got an idea.

"I'm going to plant these seeds," he said to himself. "I'm going to plant many, many seeds. I'll plant them all over America. Our land will soon be filled with apple trees." And that is just what he did.

He started a long journey. He carried a bag of apple seeds on his back. He walked north and south. He walked east and he walked west. He walked through valleys and fields. He crossed rivers and climbed mountains.

He planted apple seeds everywhere he went.

Mostly
∧ Social Studies

John Chapman gave apple seeds to everyone
he met. Soon, everyone called him Johnny Appleseed.

Today, we can still see some of the trees that Johnny
Appleseed planted. They are large, old trees filled with
apples. They are the presents he gave to his country.

A. *Answer the following questions about the story.*

1. What was Johnny Appleseed's real name?

2. Where did he live?

3. What were some of his favorite outdoor things?

4. What was Johnny's big idea?

5. When did he get his big idea?

6. What did Johnny carry on his walk?

7. Where did Johnny walk?

8. What are the presents that Johnny Appleseed gave to the United States?

B. *Think About It* - Work with a partner to answer the following questions. Write your answers down, then present them to the class.

1. What do you think Johnny's friends and family thought about his idea?
2. How did Johnny Appleseed get food to eat and find places to sleep on his long journey?
3. What states do you think Johnny Appleseed walked to if he started in Massachusetts and walked north, south, east, and west?

C. Make a two column spread sheet or chart of other fruits and vegetables that grow in the United States. In the first column put the name of the product. In the second column put the region(s) of the country where the product grows.

D. There are many other famous American folk heroes. Go to your school library and read about Paul Bunyan, Pecos Bill, Annie Oakley, or another folk hero. Write a report and present your information to your class.

Apple, Carrot, and Yogurt Salad

Here's a healthy and delicious recipe.

WHAT YOU NEED:

- $\frac{1}{4}$ teaspoon celery seed
- juice from one lemon
- dashes of salt and pepper
- 1 lb. of carrots
- 2 medium apples
- 1 cup yogurt
- 1 teaspoon honey
- $\frac{1}{2}$ cup celery stalks

1. Peel the apples. Cut them into small cubes.

2. Peel the carrots. Grate them.

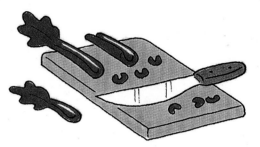

3. Cut up the celery stalks.

4. Mix in a bowl.

5. Add the lemon juice, yogurt and honey

6. Add celery seed, salt and pepper to taste.

7. Chill in the refrigerator.

8. Serve with fresh bread or crackers.

WALK AROUND THE WORLD

How long would it take to walk around the world? How many shoes would you wear out?

Well, the Earth is a pretty big place. It's about 24,804 miles around the equator. Let's say you're a speed walker, and you can walk ten miles an hour.

If you walked without stopping, it would take more than 2,480 hours – over 100 days. It would take at least ten pairs of shoes.

HOT & COLD

Here are the average temperatures in one of the coldest – and one of the hottest – cities in the USA. The temperatures are in degrees Fahrenheit.

	Jan/Feb	Mar/Apr	May/Jun	Jul/Aug	Sep/Oct	Nov/Dec
Juneau, Alaska	25	35	50	56	46	30
Miami, Florida	68	74	80	83	80	71

If you visited Juneau on your birthday, what would the temperature probably be? What would it be if you visited Miami?

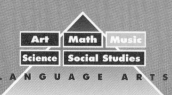

Mostly
∧ Social Studies

| Art | Math | Music |
| Science | Social Studies |

LANGUAGE ARTS

AMAZING FACTS!

● Each American tosses out about 1500 pounds of garbage every year. That's equal to the weight of one big cow.

● When your trash goes to a landfill, it doesn't decompose right away. This shows how long things last.

Paper	20-30 days
Cloth	6 months
Wood	4 years
Tin	12-15 years
Plastic	5,000 years
Glass	forever

BULLETIN BOARD

Found: Blue sweater, size large. In pocket, a bus ticket. See Mr. King in the office.

Lunch Meetings

Library - Book of the Month Club
Computer Lab - Wireheads, Inc.!
Gym - Gymnastics Team
Room 114 - Newspaper Staff

Just Joking

What happened when the baby duck flew upside down?

◆◆◆◆◆

¡dn pǝʞɔɐnb ǝH

◆◆◆◆◆

CREATIVE THINKING
A FRISBEE IS A PRETTY SIMPLE THING

In 1968, a group of high school kids in New Jersey invented a new sport around it. That sport, Ultimate Frisbee, is now played by thousands of students across the country.

Ultimate Frisbee is not unique. Every sport or game was invented by creative thinkers.

1891

Basketball invented. Twenty-one million Americans under the age of 18 now play basketball competitively.

1960's

Snowboards invented. About 600,000 snowboards are sold each year.

1968

Nerf toys invented. Nearly 100 million Nerf products have since been sold.

1980

Modern in-line skates invented. There are more than 12.5 million skaters on the road today.

1989

Nintendo Gameboy invented. More than 15 Million Gameboys and 54 million game cartridges have since been sold.

THE CENTENNIAL OLYMPIC GAMES

When – Summer, 1996, July 19 - August 4
Where – Atlanta, Georgia
Who – over 15,000 athletes and coaches
from 200 countries; over 5,000,000
TV viewers worldwide

Each Olympic Games produces new stars. Boys and girls, young men and women become medal winners – gold, silver, and bronze. Very special winners could be in an Olympic Hall of Fame. Here are two candidates.

MATT BIONDI

SWIMMING
HEIGHT: 6' 7"
WEIGHT: 210 LBS
BORN: 10/8/65. MORGANA, CA

Matt swam at three Summer Olympics (1984-92). He won eight gold medals and 11 medals in all. Matt set world records in the 50-meter and 100-meter freestyle events. He also swam on three relay teams that set world records.

WILMA RUDOLPH

TRACK AND FIELD
HEIGHT : 5'11"
WEIGHT: 130 LBS.
BORN: 6/23/40 BETHLEHEM, TENN
DIED: 11/12/94 NASHVILLE, TENN

As a kid, Wilma had polio. Polio attacks the nerves. Her left leg became partly paralyzed and twisted. She wore a brace on her leg for six years. But at the 1960 Olympics, Wilma won three gold medals. She became the first U.S. woman to earn three gold medals in track and field at one Olympics.

Who would you put in the Olympic Hall of Fame?

Outside, Inside

John Mundahl

Tough boy, I know you.
Outside, you're tough.
Tough talk.
Tough eyes.
Tough clothes.
But inside you're scared.
New country.
New people.
New faces.

Tough boy, I know you.
Outside you're tough.
Tough friends.
Tough car.
Tough walk.
But inside you're scared.
New language.
No money.
Dark skin.

Tough boy, I know you.
Take my hand,
In this strange land.
Please.
I know you.

THIS LAND IS YOUR LAND

WORDS AND MUSIC BY WOODY GUTHRIE

Chorus
This land is your land,
This land is my land,
From California,
To the New York island;
From the redwood forest,
To the Gulf Stream waters;
This land was made for you and me.

Verse 1
As I was walking
That ribbon of highway
I saw above me
That endless skyway
I saw below me,
That golden valley.
This land was made for you and me.

Chorus

Verse 2
When the sun came shining
And I was strolling
And the wheat fields waving
And the dust clouds rolling
As the fog was lifting
A voice was chanting
This land was made for you and me.

Chorus

Art | Math | Music
Science | Social Studies
LANGUAGE AR

AMAZING FACTS GAME

EACH SQUARE =
5 POINTS

THREE IN A ROW =
10 BONUS POINTS

1 Which word means "one of a kind?"
   a. unusual
   b. unique
   c. identical

2 Which holiday celebrates the American worker?
   a. Labor Day
   b. Independence Day
   c. Presidents' Day

3 Which branch of government makes the laws?
   a. Executive Branch
   b. Legislative Branch
   c. Judicial Branch

4 Where did John Chapman live?
   a. in Massachusetts
   b. in Montana
   c. in Missouri

5 Where is the Baci ceremony from?
   a. The Philippines
   b. Laos
   c. Mexico

6 Which country is in Central America?
   a. Mexico
   b. Nicaragua
   c. Vietnam

7 Which is true?
   a. The Philippines are islands in the Atlantic.
   b. Johnny Appleseed's real name was John Chapman.
   c. It's about 40,000 miles around the equator.

8 One of the coldest cities in the U.S. is
   a. Atlanta
   b. Miami
   c. Juneau

9 Which Olympic sport did Wilma Rudolph compete in?
   a. swimming
   b. track and field
   c. gymnastics

32 Mostly
   ∧ Social Studies

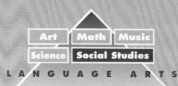

Art Math Music
Science Social Studies
LANGUAGE ARTS